# El Grupo
# McDonald's

# El Grupo McDonald's

*Poems by*
*Nick Carbó*

Tia Chucha Press
Chicago

## ACKNOWLEDGEMENTS

Grateful acknowledgment is made to the editors of those publications in
which the following poems appear:

*Asian Pacific American Journal:*
  "Día de los Difuntos," "50,000 Prostitutes Out of Work."
*The Blue Guitar:*
  "Running Amok," "El Grupo McDonald's."
*Callaloo:*
  "Votive Candles."
*Green Mountains Review:*
  "Land of the Morning."
*maganda:*
  "The Filipino Politician," "The Bronze Dove," "When the Grain is
  Golden and the Wind is Chilly Then it is the Time to Harvest."
*membrane:*
  "The Coup of 1989."
*Midland Review:*
  "Sign Language."
*Western Humanities Review:*
  "Scarborough Beach," "English As A Second Language."
*Aloud: The Nuyorican Poets Anthology* (Henry Holt):
  "The Pretty Boys of Ermita."

I would like to gratefully acknowledge the Corporation of Yaddo and
Bucknell University's Stadler Center for Poetry whose fellowships provided
time and encouragement to finish this manuscript. And thanks to those who
helped: Jane Cooper, Brooks Haxton, Thomas Lux, Patrick Pardo, Dennis
Peyton, Jeffrey Statland, Steven Styers, Jean Valentine, and Cecilia Vicuña.

Printed in the United States of America.

ISBN 1-882688-08-2
Library of Congress Catalog Card Number: 95-68620

Book Design: Jane Brunette Kremsreiter
Cover Title Photo: cyn. zarco (medium: french fries on blue astro-turf)
Cover Collage: Jane Brunette Kremsreiter
Interior Illustration: Alfonso Carbó

PUBLISHED BY:
TIA CHUCHA PRESS
*A Project of the Guild Complex*
PO Box 476969
Chicago, IL 60647

DISTRIBUTED BY:
NORTHWESTERN UNIVERSITY PRESS
*Chicago Distribution Center*
11030 S. Langley
Chicago, IL 60628

# TABLE OF CONTENTS

*for Denise*
*and my parents*

## LAND OF THE
## MORNING

Filipinas! Filipinas!

*Que noche tan oscura*
*escapaste al nacer*
*en esta madrugada*
*tan dulce con el olor*
*de Sampaguitas.*

I was born in your
October wind,
felt the breeze that rustles
Mango trees, Santol, Guava,
and Guayabano.

*Anak, taga saan ka ba?*

I grew from a seed that fell
at the foot of Mayon Volcano.
I nourished on ashes
and leftover lava.
I drank monsoon rain
in the long summers.

I had no need for clothes,
my nakedness was song
for the sun—
brown skin crescendos
from the tip of my toes
to the top of my head.

*Mis padres me encontraron*
*paseando por la selva—*
*blancos,*
*europeos,*
*como un Adonis y Venus*
*de un cuadro*
*del Renascimiento.*

I was given a language
and the emotion
of that language.
I was given a God,
whose invisible thread
is sewn to my soul.
I was given a name,
a name that has fought
for a country,
a cross,
and a king.

*Sino ba ang tunay na Filipino?*
*Ang Bontoc, ang Ifugao, ang Negrito,*
*ang Tasaday, ang Maranaw? Sino?*

I am the names of my land—
Manila, Cebu, Zamboanga,
Luzon, Visayas, and Mindanao.

Filipinas!
Filipinas!

# Part 1

......................

"...that's the secret of enduring life;
to face death, sickness, injustice, fear,
and to say:
It's a game, my heart, a game, don't be afraid."

—Nikos Kazantzakis

# LITTLE BROWN BROTHER

I've always wanted to play the part
of that puckish pubescent Filipino boy

in those John Wayne Pacific-War movies.
Pepe, Jose, or Juanito would be smiling,

bare-chested and eager to please
for most of the steamy jungle scenes.

I'd be the one who would cross
the Japanese lines and ask for tanks,

air support, or more men. I'd miraculously
make it back to the town where John Wayne

is holding his position against the enemy
with his Thompson machine-gun. As a reward,

he'd rub that big white hand on my head
and he'd promise to let me clean

his Tommy gun by the end of the night. But
then, a Betty Grable look-a-like love

interest would divert him by sobbing
into his shoulder, saying how awfully scared

she is about what the "Japs" would do
to her if she were captured. In one swift

motion, John Wayne would sweep her off
her feet to calm her fears inside his private quarters.

Because of my Hollywood ability

to be anywhere, I'd be under the bed

watching the woman roll down her stockings
as my American hero unbuckles his belt.

I'd feel the bottom of the bed bounce off my chest
as small-arms fire explodes outside the walls.

## THE BOY IN BLUE SHORTS

The screaming woman on the other side
of our tall black gate
would have thrown a rock at me.
My maid, Rosita, sheltered me from the insults—
      something about my being
      retarded and full of worms.

The woman nudged her son forward.
Blue shorts, clean T-shirt, rubber slippers.
She said her little boy was the one
who should have been adopted, he was healthy.
He was about my age,
four or five. We were both silent.
*I want to see the Mr. and the Mrs.,*
*they are making a big mistake.*

Rosita bolted the gate, took me by the hand—
*they are bad people, don't listen to them.*
I felt the crisp whiteness of her skirt all the way across
the garden, back to our house.

## AT FIVE, WHILE EXPLORING THE CREEK BEHIND MY HOUSE

A group of children saw me
standing on the other side.
They stopped their game
of *patintero*.
A boy and a girl walked
across the coconut bridge,
urged me to cross over
and play with them.
The barefoot boy,
and then the girl
negotiated the narrow trunk.

I took two steps
and almost slipped.
The children across the creek
screamed I should remove
my shoes
because the bridge
was slippery.
I jumped back to the bank,
noticed they were all barefoot,
they were still urging me on.

I was afraid of falling
and would not leave
my new leather shoes
behind.
Without waving good bye,
I ran home,
past our barbed-wire fence
the one with the bright red
bougainvilleas.

## IN TAGALOG IBON MEANS BIRD

Carmencita said I had a small ibon
hiding between my legs. I was eight years old,

smiling at our three maids eating
their dinner of dried salted fish and warm white rice.

My parents were out at the Adamsons'
for cocktails, red snapper, or mahi-mahi.

It was a Friday night when Carmencita asked if I could show
the ibon inside my pajamas. *Hold him tight*

*so he won't fly away.* I felt a small stirring—
anticipating a sudden flutter of wings

like the little brown birds that would fly
past my window in the morning. *Look,*

*your ibon must be hungry, feed him*
*some of this rice, and watch, he will grow.*

I watched my ibon peck at the white grains
offered by her outstretched palm. His belly grew fat

but he was not really eating. Maybe he wanted
some kind of seeds, peanuts, or a little water.

*Your ibon is very pretty, his lips are red, one day he will sing*
*to a beautiful woman and she will fall in love*

*with your ibon and she will kiss him all night long.*
Carmencita, Nora, and Rosita giggled to each other

as they told me to hide my agitated ibon
because he was about to escape. I went back

to my room hungrier than when I woke up.

## DIA DE LOS DIFUNTOS

*(San Agustin Church, Intramuros)*

All the bones of old Manila
are here: Achaval, Ayala, Eduardo,
Cacho, Garchitorena, Garcia,
Melian, Nieto, Prieto, Preysler,
Soriano, Valdez, Zobel.
*Los nombres de buenas familias,*
whose descendants speak Spanish
amongst themselves. Their maids carry
baskets of fresh daisies and carnations.
My mother spots a Roxas she knew
from school. They greet each other
in Spaglish: "Estás maravillosa!
Have you been on a diet, mujer?
How are the children y el esposo?"

My father's father is on the top row
of graves on the west wall.
I've never met him except in a few
black and white photographs.
Don Alfonso in his *Cuerpo de Voluntarios
del Casino Español* uniform, in 1898.
In his right hand, the single action Mauser
he surrendered to Commodore Dewey's
American forces when they took Manila.
Don Alfonso in an all-white suit
at the Boulevard in 1921 with my father
at eight years old, holding
his father's hand.

On the north wall we find Maria Luisa,
my father's sister, among a list of people
massacred by the Japanese in 1945.
She was pregnant at the time,

the soldiers shot into the room
full of women, bayonetted
the ones left alive. I leave a small
bouquet of flowers—*plastic,*
*because they last longer.*

## EL GRUPO McDONALD'S

My father is seventy-seven and meets
with a group of "old-timers"
every other day in a McDonald's
in the heart of Makati.
These men have worked
for the prestigious firms of Soriano,
Ayala, and Elizalde. Accountants,
Managing Vice-Presidents, District
Consultants, and Sales Representatives.
A white long-sleeved shirt, white trousers,
and a black leather belt is the dress code
for these retired *Ilustrados*.

The coffee is always hot and *los temas
de conversación son, las bases Americanas,
el cambio del Dollar, la Cory Aquino,
y el tiempo distante cuando Manila
era la perla del oriente.*
The city is changing color, fresh air
from the bay does not blow into Makati
and the pollution lingers all night.

My father tells me that Enrique,
the ex-Jai-alai star, died
over the summer, Ralph Zulueta is also dead.
He tells me that even if the group is shrinking
every year, they still talk about the idiots
in the government, the American bases,
the exchange rate of the Dollar, Cory Aquino,
and the days when Manila was still
the pearl of the orient.

# CIVILIZING THE FILIPINO

*"I find this work very monotonous,*
*trying to teach these monkeys to talk.*
*The more I see of this lazy, dirty, indolent people,*
*the more I come to despise them. I am becoming*
*more and more convinced that for years and years*
*to come, the only business Americans ought to have*
*over here is to rule them with severity."*
        *—Harry Cole, teacher on the island of Leyte, 1903*


I remember the time I was called
to the Principal's Office
in fourth grade. I was accused

by Kevin Stapleton of stealing
his gold Parker pen.
The American principal grabbed me

by the cuffs of my shirt,
called me a "dirty, lying Filipino"
when I told him I was not the one

who stole the pen.
That was the first time I learned
about brute force, about how the color

of my skin makes me a more likely
suspect for a crime, about how it feels
to be picked up by two white

fists and thrown to the ground.
I cried, said I had stolen
the gold pen and that I had lost it

in the playground. The principal said
my parents had to buy Kevin
a new pen or pay for its replacement.

The next day I went straight
to the office with two hundred pesos.
I was ashamed that I lied to my parents

about why I needed the money,
ashamed that I was too scared
to tell the truth

about my innocence,
ashamed that I had become
a dirty, lying Filipino.

# HILOT, CURANDERA, WITCH

*for Lucille Clifton*

I.
he was not breathing–

when I was eight years old, my little brother fell
from the guava tree in front of our house

his eyes were closed–

mother was hysterical and she began to scream
she pushed me away
people opened their doors and windows

Felipe was not moving–

I suddenly felt his body was my body
felt I was inside him
I knew his soul was still there
and I prayed to God
to let him live

his mouth suddenly began to cough–

mother stopped crying, she told me
to help her
I put my hands on Felipe's body
to stroke his pain away, to awaken his soul

Felipe said mother's name–

the neighbors said it was a miracle

II.
soon after, a man brought his sick dog
to the house asking me to cure it
I didn't know what to do
but I took the dog's drooping head
and a voice told me to look
inside the dog's mouth
there was a chicken bone stuck
in its throat

then people kept coming to our house
asking me to pray
for them and put my small hands
on their foreheads, necks, stomachs
or backs to take away their pain
they said I was blessed by God

III.
my mother took me to the village priest
he said my gifts could not be called
miracles, they were just manifestations
of our faith in God
he said if I did this too often
my health would be endangered

my mother forbade me from seeing
any more sick people

IV.
when I married, I became friendly
with my husband's aunt who knew
how to cure
she knew I had the gift and told me
I should cure people again

I learned the right prayers
I learned how to bless the water
I learned which herbs to use
I learned the illnesses and their symptoms
I learned how to remove demons
from people's sick bodies
I felt my old powers returning

V.
my husband went to Manila to find work
he never came back
some neighbors said he found
another woman, some said he's in jail

I lit candles to all the Saints, prayed
to find the truth
a voice said that God had taken
my husband away, that he was now at peace
that my new obligation in life
was to cure the people who came to my door

VI.
two months ago, four men
who said they were from the New People's Army
came to my house
one of them was wounded,
I saw they had honest faces, so I said
I would help them

I took ylang-ylang leaves and rubbed
them on the wound
then a bullet came out

they said I was a hero of the proletarian people
but I didn't know what those words meant

VII.

my name is Alicia Gaspar, I am a healer
I was given this gift from God
to help good people
I have no children, I am not afraid
of jails, of soldiers

I want to find the bones of my husband
because he comes to me in my dreams
he tells me he is so cold there
and he needs to come back
to the place where I can offer
him prayers
and the smoke of the petals
of the white gumamelas

I am a hilot
I am telling the truth

## RUNNING AMOK

In the slums of Tondo, people dwell
in shacks of cardboard, bits of bamboo,
corrugated metal, and a few cement blocks.

They come from all the provinces—
a farmer's son from Cagayan,
a coal miner from Bulacan,

a field hand from the banana plantations
of Davao. They come to Manila
for work, for better pay.

The highest incidence of men
running amok is in Tondo,
or at least, that's what the local tabloids

have for headlines every week. *Amok in Tondo
kills seven! Police shoot him to death!*
During the Filipino-American War

from 1899 to 1902, the Colt .45 pistol
was *refined* to kill crazed
Moro fighters who ran amok

and would not stop attacking
with rabid animal urgency
when shot with bullets of lesser caliber.

The superstitious old women in Tondo say
that no rice, no shoes, and no work
breed beetles and violence.

They say that small black beetles
can lay eggs in a man's ear,
and this is what makes a man run.

# "WHEN THE GRAIN IS GOLDEN AND THE WIND IS CHILLY, THEN IT IS THE TIME TO HARVEST"

*Leron-leron sinta, umakyat sa papaya*
*Dala-dala'y buslo', sisidlan ng bunga**

In a dusty village in Cagayan Valley,
Ramon and his father were planting rice when soldiers

appeared on their farm. They questioned his father,
if he'd seen any communist rebels recently

in the area, and when he did not give them
a good enough answer, they beat him with the blunt ends

of their rifles, shot him as he was lying
on the ground. Ramon snuck away but remained hidden

in nearby bushes, to witness the soldiers
laugh out loud as they chopped his father's shaking body—

*"they first removed his penis, then cut below*
*the knees, then the ankles, then the elbows, then the neck."*

*Leron-leron sinta, umakyat sa papaya*
*Dala-dala'y buslo', sisidlan ng bunga*

---

*The first two lines of a Filipino folk song children sing while they
are playing.

This poem is derived from events retold by the Director of the
Children's Rehabilitation Center in Manila in an interview in
*The Philippines: Fire on the Rim*, pp. 296-299, edited by Joseph Collins
(The Institute for Food and Development Policy 1989, San Francisco, CA).

After dusk Ramon ran home to his mother
and younger brother. She feared the soldiers would soon
   knock

on their door, so she took her sons deep inside
the muddy jungle of the Sierra Madre mountains.

After about four weeks, she sent Ramon to buy
rice, some fish, and a few canned goods. The sun was heavy,

the road to the village kept stretching further
and his legs felt weak, so Ramon boarded a jeepney

to take him to the market on Luna street.
A soldier recognized him at a military

checkpoint and he pointed his gun at Ramon,
yelled at him to step out with his hands up in the air.

*Leron-leron sinta, umakyat sa papaya*
*Dala-dala'y buslo', sisidlan ng bunga*

No questions were asked. Ramon told us the most
painful torture he endured was when the soldiers joined

two blocks of wood and used the weapon to hit
him directly on the ears, over and over

until he bled. He doesn't remember how
he escaped but he found himself wandering around

the countryside for many days, eating grass,
guava leaves, bamboo shoots, and bananas to survive.

*Leron-leron sinta, umakyat sa papaya*
*Dala-dala'y buslo', sisidlan ng bunga*

Here, at the Children's Rehabilitation
Center, Ramon made friends, played with the other children,

started to learn how to write. He asked questions
about his mother and younger brother, he wanted

to know when he could return to his village
to harvest their rice fields. He said it was important

to go home because "*when the grain is golden
and the wind is chilly, then it is the time to harvest.*"

After four months, we learned that Ramon's mother
was probably dead. *"Where's the body? I want to see*

*the body, I want to bury my mother.*"
I told him we didn't know where the body was, but we

would try to find it. After a long silence,
he finally went to his room. Then I followed him

upstairs, found him hunched over the bathroom sink
washing his red face again and again and again.

*Leron-leron sinta, umakyat sa papaya
Dala-dala'y buslo', sisidlan ng bunga*

Ramon is still with us, his friends have brought him
out of his shell, he has learned how to speak Tagalog,

and he is beginning to read. Ramon dreams
about going home. He writes letters to his younger

brother even though we tell him he is still
missing. We collect those letters he writes every day.

He tells his younger brother, *"If you come here,*
*you will have many good friends to play with, eat plenty*

*of food, and these nice people will let us stay*
*here in Manila, but maybe I will go home first*

*and see what's happened to our family farm."*
He then writes, *"Do you know that your mother is now dead?"*

# Part 2

*"Sometimes we must look at things
with innocence, gentleness."*

C.P. Cavafy

## AMERICAN ADOBO

She showed up on the doorstep of my apartment
in Albuquerque just after the blizzard of '85
in a fluffy tan fake-fur coat, an elevated

*I Love Lucy* hairdo, and a twelve-year-old son.
I was honored to be given the front passenger seat
of her 1976 Datsun while her son aimed

his pink plastic water pistol from the back.
Her two-bedroom duplex was nestled in the foothills
of the rust-covered Sandia mountains.

The hug back at the apartment was genuine—
my older cousin, Nancy, her son, Alfonso,
named after my father. This was a chance to ignite

memories from familiar names, to recuperate
the fallen leaves of our family tree, to run
back to our childhoods, separated

by two continents and an ocean.
She said she still believes
that "the Carbó's are blue-blood,

a royalty from Spain." Nobody
could take that away from her—the promise
of gold crowns, swords forged

from Toledo steel with the Carbó name
glimmering on the blade. I didn't tell her
that the only title our grandfather carried

was that of *Perito Mercantil Colegiado*, a Certified
Public Accountant. I didn't tell her that the only

time he ruled the masses was as the Vice-Mayor

of the provincial town of Nueva Caceres.
"In 1956, when I was nine,
your mother and your father came to visit

our house on Losoya Street—they came out
of a black limousine, they looked so regal,
so elegant, they brought so many gifts."

She was standing by the microwave fluffing
a pot of Uncle Ben's Minute Rice
while I reviewed her family album on the couch

which was covered with a multi-colored
Mexican blanket. I understood the story
in black and white—

her American father left them in 1954,
my aunt Nana learned to change sheets
in motels on Central Avenue and serve coffee

at diners to earn enough money
for three children. When Nana died in 1982,
Nancy was the only child to sit by her bed.

"This was my mother's special recipe
for beef and pork adobo. She cooked it
for us on Thanksgiving and Easter Sunday."

I didn't tell Nancy that her adobo
was too watery, that it needed more soy sauce,
that it should have had more garlic.

# THE COUP OF DECEMBER 1989

The day after Andres Bonifacio Day
(All Heroes Day, November 30),
several troops of the New Philippine Army
marched into the heart of Makati.
They occupied the Intercontinental Hotel,
the Urdaneta Condominiums,
one of the Twin Towers,
the Manila Gardens Hotel,
the Atrium Office Building,
and the Green Belt Shopping Mall.
For six days, my parents never
went close to a window,
never turned their lights on at night,
never dared to go out into the street.
My father would describe the gunshots,
the impact of bullets
hitting their apartment terrace
while we were talking on the phone.
I could hear the M-16's firing in the background.
I knew where the rebels were shooting from
and from where the government soldiers
were returning their fire.
I was watching the coup on CNN
in San Antonio, Texas—fed this information
long distance to my father.
On December 8, the rebel soldiers surrendered.
My father said nobody got hurt
except a maid on the sixth floor
of our apartment building.
*She peered from her bathroom window*
*and spotted soldiers on the roof*
*of the Green Belt Mall parking lot.*
*They saw her head*
*and she quickly ducked.*

*After a few minutes, she stuck her head
out again and that's when the sniper
shot her.*

# THE BRONZE DOVE

*for Marty Lopez*

1. BENIGNO AQUINO JR. INTERNATIONAL AIRPORT

The adobe-brown terminal looms
like a sleeping *carabao* caked with mud—

you come up with fifty words to describe
the different shades of green you saw
rushing up from the ground,
you scratch your neck, feel the grime and sweat
from San Francisco or L.A. on your nape,
you look out your window seat
search for a plaque or a stain of blood—
this is the tarmac where he was shot.

(For a better view, go to Ayala Avenue in Makati.
In front of the Bank of the Philippine Islands
and the Insular Life Building is the statue
with the stairs and the dove on his shoulder.
While you're there, look
for the statues of Lapu Lapu and Tandang Sora
among the ipil-ipil trees on Makati Avenue.)

You pass through a fluorescent-white curtain
of warm air as you descend
into the unloading tube—
a smile from an airline attendant,
the long walk to the Immigration booth,

*Balikbayan sir? Welcome home.*

a stamp for six months on your US passport,
another ten-dollar bill between its pages
for the Customs people up ahead,

*Balikbayan? Do you have anything to declare,*
*pasalubong, expensive gifts*
*for the relatives? Thank you sir!*

a porter in a red shirt takes your luggage
to the street level, asks for five dollars,
the faces of a hundred people pressed
behind a bamboo fence stare
as you board a Golden or Metro taxi cab.

You inhale the humid air, sweat is now
running down your face.


2. E. DE LOS SANTOS AVENUE

The Jeepnies are engorged with eight
or ten passengers, each jeepney
speeding and stopping with their fiesta
of sounds, of colors, the bodies inside
breathing carbon monoxide.

You take the overpass into Makati—
to the right is the long tan wall topped
with barbed-wire hiding the luxury homes
of Dasmarinas Village, to the left
is San Lorenzo Village where you'll find
the San Lorenzo Pre-school.
Go to the house in Zulueta Circle,
this is where the poet
of *Like The Molave* once lived.
His widow's name is Cora.

On the corner of Edsa and Buendia,
among the street vendors selling
copies of *Woman's Day, Manila Bulletin,*

or Marlboro and Winston cigarettes,
you might see a girl without a left arm tapping
on windows of stopped cars pointing
to her mouth, asking for money.
Every other year, before the monsoon rains,
it's the same arm that's cut off
just above the elbow, a different
young face running up to cars
in the same intersection.


### 3. CAMP CRAME AND CAMP AGUINALDO

You pass Camp Crame where Ninoy Aquino,
Jose Maria Sison, the poet Mila D. Aguilar,
and countless others were "detained"
under Marcos. The positive wire
attatched to the penis, the negative
to the scrotum. This is also the place
where more than a million people
said "no" to the Dictator. You may still
hear stories about the tear gas,
the armored personnel vehicles,
the ordinary people who would not
move out of the way. They say
that for three days the electricity
to the whole city was turned off
but the people still fought for freedom,
sang songs to each other around bonfires,
made love by candlelight.

# THE FILIPINO POLITICIAN

When he finds his wife in bed with another man—

The conservative politician feels an ache in his stomach,
   remembers the *longanisa* and the *tapa* he had for breakfast.
He doesn't know whether to get the doctor or Cardinal Sin
   on the phone. He calls one of his bodyguards, tells him
to shoot the man and then, his wife. He takes his .38
      magnum
   from his brief case, shoots his bodyguard in the back.

The liberal politician pours himself a glass of Courvoisier,
   remembers a passage from an Anais Nin story.
He is suddenly the one they call *the Basque.* He removes
   his Dior tie, his Armani shirt, his Calvin Klein boxer
      shorts.
He puts on a black beret, whispers, *tres jolie, tres jolie,*
   *que bonito, muy grande* my *petite amore.* He joins them
in bed, begins his caresses on the man's calves,
   kisses his way up the man's thighs.

The communist politician does not call his wife a *puta,*
   nor does he challenge the man to a duel with *balisong*
      knives.
He stays calm, takes out a book of poems by Mao Tse Tung.
   Inspired, he decides to advance the Revolution.
He takes a taxi to Roxas Boulevard, he begins to curse
   and throw rocks at the American Embassy.

# THE PRETTY BOYS OF ERMITA

Lately, they've been offering
the *Mt. Pinatubo Special.*
Ten and thirteen-year-old boys
promise that their tongues
can make a man's penis feel
seismic twitches.
Customers have come from Australia,
Scandinavia, and even America
for these tourist attractions.
They arrive from across the globe
in pre-paid packaged tours.
Their brochures advertise
nude boys frolicking
under an orange sunset,
on a white sand beach.
The first stop is a bar in Ermita
where these white men pair off
with the brown boy
of their choice. After an evening
of volcanic experiences,
the men and the boys are bused
to a "private" beach resort in the south,
for a week of sun, sex, and piña coladas.
On the back of the brochure,
a man from Sydney claims
that it was the best vacation
he's ever had.

I wonder if a middle-aged man
in Berlin, Stockholm, or New York
is looking through a set of pictures
of the pretty boys of Ermita.
I wonder if that man is holding
his white penis in his hand,

thinking of how those boys
are growing into men,
wondering if Jose, Tito,
or Eddie are still alive.

# "50,000 PROSTITUTES OUT OF WORK"

from an article in Ms. MAGAZINE
July/August 1992

Some of the older women line
the roads overlooking Subic Bay
as the last American ships pull
out from the naval base.
Mabel is sixty-seven, remembers
the happiness she felt at twenty
when the Americans returned
to Olongapo after World War II.
They paid well, brought her stockings
from New York and San Francisco,
a few sailors even offered
to marry her.
Mabel has a nineteen-year-old
granddaughter, Marissa, who began
working at fifteen. She made
enough money to support her mother
and three younger brothers.
Marissa has survived syphilis twice,
has been pregnant only once.
The American sailor promised
to take her back to South Carolina,
but left her with only a letter
and a hundred dollars.
Mabel does not wave at the ships—
they have taken their flag down
for the last time—a frigate,
three destroyers, a floating dry-dock,
and an aircraft carrier.
Mabel worries about Marissa—
she has gone to Manila looking for work.
After four months, still no letters,

no money for the family.
Mabel does not know what to do—
nobody looks at her body anymore
as she walks the streets
of Olongapo wearing
her dry black dress.

# MARISSA

*'You must die'—but is that so distressing?*
*You just feel slightly sick,*
*As you enter the stain on the wall.*
*    —Irina Ratushinskaya*

In a dark cubicle with a mattress smelling
of dried semen, she takes fifty pesos
for the blindfold, another fifty for the strap
of leather that the foreigner will use
to bind her wrists. It will be strong enough to hang
her from the wall.
                         Marissa waits outside
the Pink Paradise night club for her grandmother.
American sailors passing by ask
her, *how much.* They think her school uniform is just
a costume dreamed up by the club's owner.
Marissa remembers how her grandmother first
taught her the technique for the Peso Show—

*See, you get many men to donate all the coins*
*they can spare. Stack them six, seven, or eight*
*inches high, pour some beer over the pesos, take*
*a deep breath and slowly lower yourself*
*over the stack. Always look straight into the eyes*
*of the sailors who gave you their coins, keep*
*smiling as you walk to the bathroom to empty*
*sixty or more pesos into your palms.*

The foreigner has Marissa's thighs wrapped around
his waist, her back pressed against the wall.
She hears loud music playing downstairs, Madonna
or Michael Jackson—girls dancing, waiting
to get picked.

She feels her grandmother's hand combing
her long hair, wiping sweat from her forehead.
She sees her grandmother in a black dress leaving
for work. Remembers thinking of her as
the most beautiful woman in Olongapo.
She does not feel her hands, the pulse inside
her wrists.
                    She's already a cold piece of the wall.

# HOBBIT HOUSE

*"...is at 1801 Mabini St., has a good international atmosphere and the
dubious attraction of waiters who are all dwarfs."*
    *—Guide Book, May 1991*

*I learned how to make love in Paris, Florence,
and Alexandria.* She was not taller than a ten-year-old
Shirley Temple, her cherubic hand fit perfectly
around the miniature bottle of San Miguel Beer. I pictured
the paintings of the renaissance—the Tintorettos,
the Caravaggios, and the Titians. I connected
that face with the kind of body which only the Masters
saw as belonging to those of angels, then she asked
my name and my favorite color. Stuart and cerulean blue.

*You look like a Michael J. Fox but with more muscles
and a fine dark beard.* I ordered us another round,
told her that I was in Manila for business—sheet metal—
that the travel agency in Seattle had suggested this bar
as the likeliest place to find the most beautiful small women
of these seven thousand islands. That night, she showed me
the sights of Paris, Florence, and Alexandria. And her name
was Angelina.

# Part 3

*"That's it. The lover writes, the believer hears,
the poet mumbles and the painter sees,
each one, his fated eccentricity."*

*–Wallace Stevens*

# FILIPINO JOE

I'm afraid to go back there. I would be just as surprised
at all the changes if I'd walk into my apartment and find
the sofa missing and a large Labrador wagging his loud tail

at me in its place. The names of streets have been known
to change with whoever happens to be in power.
Is Imelda Boulevard still on the jeepney run

between Baclaran and EDSA?
Does the Goldilocks bakery on Mabini Street still make
the best *ensaymadas* in Manila? Can I order a whole roasted

chicken at Max's Restaurant in Ermita and not pay more
than fifty pesos? I've been told that Tia Maria's,
the smokey Mexican restaurant just up the street

from where I went to high school has moved
to Makati Avenue. For twenty pesos, my friends and I had
San Miguel beer and burritos after our classes.

At night we met at Andros, the bar in Greenbelt
that never asked for identification and played the first
MTV videos of Adam Ant, Kaja Goo Goo,

and the Human League. Am I dating myself?
Those were the pre-people power days
when money was flying out of the country faster

than the Monkey-Eating Eagle could swoop into a grove
of balete trees and grab a squealing Tarsier from its branches
just before it fell to the illegal loggers who sold the logs

to Japan where the wood was made into toothpicks.
Does that sentence make any sense? At this very moment
I'm chewing on a nice round Made-in-America

wooden toothpick because I've just quit
nine years of smoking and I need something to keep
my mouth busy while I try my hardest to finish this poem.

I smoked my first stick in Manila. It was an imported
R.J. Reynolds cigarette. One pack and I was hooked.
It's Nicotine Imperialism—the Marlboro Man rode

into town and spread his addictive habit. If I remember
right, he was everywhere—in the movie houses, on sides
of buildings, under bridges, in dirty bathrooms

(now, that will never change), on tote bags,
on kitchen utensils, and even the corridors
of local cancer wards. I'm afraid to go back.

I've heard the cigarette vendors on the streets
have multiplied like gnats and they now pester you
with two-free-for-one-stick deals.

I'm afraid that when I step off the plane, I'll be greeted
by an effigy of Joe Camel wagging his tail at me
with a placard above his head saying WELCOME BACK

TO MANILA JOE. WE LOVE YOU JOE.

# MAEGDEN, YOUNG WOMAN,
# OR YAYA

What if all the maids in Manila were manumitted
by a special Presidential Decree? All over the city
those little silver and brass bells would ring
in unison and every maid from Aida to Zita
would not answer the Señora's call. The houses
would gather dust balls in the corners, plants
would wither, and those three-inch red roaches
would invade the living room because the Señora
couldn't find where they kept the insect repellent.
The bed sheets that used to be washed and ironed
every other day would stink by the end of the week,
and the *kintab na kintab* shine of the hardwood floors
would stop reflecting the bald head of Mr. Clean.
In the kitchen, the Señora would face four kilos
of fresh squid for *adobong pusit* and it would be
the first time she shoves her finger inside
something that used to be alive. The phone rings
as she begins to pull out the squid's intestines
and she picks it up with her slimy left hand
while she frantically tries to shake off the tentacles
that have cupped themselves to her right. She repeats
the greeting she required her maids to memorize.
*Hello, this is the Coronado residence*
*in Forbes Park, good morning, buenos días,*
*and magandang umaga po, how may I help you.*
It's her best friend and majong partner
in Dasmariñas Village,
*Ay na'ko, Lydia, have your maids manumitted also?*
*What the calchichas does manumitted mean?*
The Señora wipes the back of her hand
on her hair and the tentacles stick to her forehead,

*Quien sabe Cora, it was the Presidente, he likes to use*
*those complicated words like, sequester, munificent,*
*and remuneration. He said Filipinos have become too dependent*
*on their maids. Can you imagine that, Cora?*
The Señora finds a spatula,
scrapes off the squid from her forehead and stuffs it down
the trash disposal. Her friend's voice is barely audible
over the grinding noise—*Lydia, are you cooking tonight*
*or going out to a restaurant again?* The Señora reaches
for the small silver bell, rings it just to listen
to the sound—*Shakey's Pizza,*
*it's the only place in Manila where we can get served*
*without feeling guilty. But Cora, I have to make*
*a reservation for tonight. The place is going to be packed.*

# PRAYERS TO THE
# VIRGIN OF ANTIPOLO

*"People leave personal notes at the foot of this statue
looking for miracles. It's like a parish newspaper.
I know all the headlines."*
       *—Father Rigoberto*

Holy Mother, Rico did not come home in the plane
         from Romblon, please make sure he's still alive.
Holy Mother, my Toyota broke down four days ago,
         I need seven hundred pesos for a new carburetor.
Holy Mother, I promise to lay wreaths of Sampaguitas
         on your altar every day if you cure
         my daughter's abscess liver.
Holy Mother, please help my husband stop
         seeing his mistresses.
Holy Mother, let my father receive a big raise
         so he can afford my scuba-diving lessons.
Holy Mother, Estella won't have sex with me anymore,
         she says she's busy praying to you every night.
Holy Mother, my son needs eyeglasses
         and a pair of brand new blue jeans.
Holy Mother, I will stop nagging my husband
         about his mistresses if you let me get pregnant.
Holy Mother, pray for Jesse, Rolando, and Carlita,
         they were killed in a car crash in Baguio.
Holy Mother, please give my sister, Rosario, another day
         without the pain inside her bones.
Holy Mother, uncle Arturo has touched me
         between my legs again. Please make him stop.
Holy Mother, Sarah has not eaten in six days,
         we don't know what to do.
Holy Mother, my mistress is threatening to tell my wife
         about our secret meetings at the Hotel Tropicana
         unless I buy her a new car.

Holy Mother, thank you for curing my mother's colon
    cancer. She's coming home in two weeks
    for her grand-daughter's birthday.
Holy Mother, uncle Arturo was taken to jail yesterday.

# CAPTIVA

*"Both young and old males pierce their penises with a gold or tin rod
the size of a goose quill, its ends shaped like the head of a nail . . .
When a man and a woman wish to have intercourse, she takes his penis
not in the normal way, but gently introduces first the top spur
and then the bottom one into her vagina. Once inside,
the penis becomes erect and cannot be withdrawn until it is limp."*
   *—Antonio Pigafetta,
    on the sexual practices of Filipino natives, 1521*


The women of Mactaan knew they could not trust
those penises. They learned from their sisters,
mothers, and grandmothers that even the largest ones

would lie, talk their way out of having to linger
inside those warm slippery walls.
The men always had something else to do—

finish hollowing out the *banca* so the men could go
fishing in a new boat, pick more coconuts
to make enough *arak,* (a palm wine the men made

to get drunk together.) Tying the men to the furniture
took too much time, biting them
as they were pulling out was considered too violent,

threatening to cut it off with a bamboo knife
never worked. Then, the women of Mactaan heard
of a secret sexual practice from a shaman

visiting from an island to the south.
They introduced the gold penis rod
to their pubescent boys as a ritual

to attain manhood. It took twenty days
for their penises to heal, three years

before these boys began to please the women.

The older men, who laughed
at this younger generation,
(calling them *ulo ng aspili,* pin heads)

were gradually seen as unattractive
by their wives and younger women.
The unadorned men were accused

of ejaculating too fast, not keeping
their penises swollen long enough,
having bad breath, balding prematurely, warts.

No woman would touch these unpierced men.
One day, the village elders and the rest
of the nervous adult men lined up

in front of the old woman's hut who performed
this service. In twenty days,
all the men of Mactaan had penises that sparkled

when exposed to the sun.
They walked around with their chests out,
enjoying freshly made *arak,*

while the women wondered if *two,*
or maybe *three* gold rods would increase
their pleasure and propel them

past the tops of palm trees,
past the shimmering eyes of the gods
in the evening sky.

# ON THE ISLAND OF MINDORO

Around the towns of Calapan, Naujan, Pinamalayan,
and San Jose, they say a special mushroom grows
on the excrement of the water buffalo.

In a myth explained by the locals,
the water buffalo was sent to them
by the spirits of the land.

The *carabao* is worth more
than a car to a farmer, it takes three *carabaos*
to win a bride, they can never be killed for food.

The locals have been known
to harvest the mushrooms that grow
from the excrement of the *carabao*.

They believe it's a gift
to make them see and hear
the spirits of fields,

of forests,
of dark evenings.
They eat the mushrooms,

mix them with new rice and cane sugar.
They sit on their wooden porches
and stare at the distance just after dusk.

# TUYO

*"I just spoke to Villa on the phone last night and will see him before the end of the week. He asked me to buy some live crabs and "tuyo" in Chinatown for him. He loves the stuff."*
  —Luis Cabalquinto
  (from a letter dated 24 March '94)

The fisherman in Rizal Beach sold us crabs that were as big
as the hubcaps of our '67 Pontiac. I remember
their coffee-colored claws were tied with abaca rope.

Those pincers could have cut through my arm
if I had stuck my hand inside the salt-water bucket.
The fresh water in the large pot had to be boiling hard

before the crabs could be thrown in. I remember the hiss
and the slow dying whistle coming from inside the pot
and when I turned towards the ocean, I easily mistook

that sound as human screams carried by the Pacific wind.
That was in Bicol where Mayon volcano first greets the sun
sent by our relatives in San Francisco and New York—

a *pasalubong* for every day.
The crabs you find in Chinatown will be smaller
than the fist you made when you first heard

of your father's death. Despite their small size,
these crabs will hiss louder than the passing siren
of the EMS ambulance outside

your New York apartment window. I remember
the fisherman in Rizal Beach had two fingers missing.
It happened when he was still a boy

when he stuck his hand in a dark hole
under a coral reef. He said the crabs were even bigger
in those days. Nobody heard him scream.

## VOTIVE CANDLES
*for Denise*

I tell my mother my girlfriend is a good Catholic girl—
every Wednesday, she lights electric votive candles
in Our Lady of Guadalupe Church on 14th Street.

She prays that I don't leave her, that no one
mugs me on the way home, that the electricity used
to light the candles doesn't waste energy

and increase our country's dependence on foreign oil.
She has pictures of the Virgin Mary on the wall
in the hallway to her studio. Below these pictures

is a rack of plastic, brass, and pewter jewelry.
She says that the Virgin protects her,
that her apartment was robbed twelve times

and they never stole her earrings, bracelets,
and necklaces. She writes about her desire
for Catholic school girls to become

Popes or Presidents. She hopes someday a woman
will run the Vatican, will legalize all forms
of contraception and be the first to take

a pro-choice stance against male-dominated
governments. My mother asks me if my girlfriend
has ever been to confession. I tell her that she has had

the first and a few others, but what really matters
is that she writes confessional poetry,
that the whole world can be the judge of her sins,

mortal or venial. My mother says she'll pray for us,
light two real candles in the chapel
for the Perpetual Help of Jesus.

## THE VISIT

Your presence
invented the room—

the light of translucent
chalcedony

through the window,
the sudden scent

of camphor, the bed sheets
breathing.

You closed the door
behind you

to give me the instant
and its memory.

You parted my lips
with your smile,

and I swallowed your
phosphorescence, there.

# SCARBOROUGH BEACH

*for Denise*

Early the next day, we found
two men with metal detectors
scanning the beach for earrings,
bracelets, coins, anything silver,
gold, or platinum. You told me
how your sister, Michele, lost
her wedding-band and how she searched
the floor of her car, the pipe
under the sink, the insides of her two
daughters' mouths. She was afraid
her husband would hit her, maybe
refuse to speak to her for a month.

The detector must have indicated gold—
the man was hunched on one knee,
his terrier barking at the spot
as if a dead animal or bone
were under the sand. You said her husband
bought her another ring, made love
to her that evening, making it seem
as if it were the first time their bodies
could lose themselves again and again.

# "ANSWER ME. DANCE MY DANCE."
*—Muriel Rukeyser*

I've kept the envelopes closed,
corners bent over the back

of the couch where I first learned
the language of her wrists.

Those hands, she said,
were not mine when they climbed

the sides of your face.
The touch, my feeling of vertigo

when she looked down,
not touching me

there, until I untied
her feelings for her husband.

She was more than an acrobat,
a contortionist, she could

dismember her body
and present me with just

her breasts one evening,
soles of her feet a week later.

I have photographs of her
almost whole, on the day

she ended the affair,
when she left me her soft

red tongue attached
to my sleeve.

## SIGN LANGUAGE

I saw you over
my martini glass, engaged
in a conversation

using your hands. It seemed
as though each word were a bird
that fluttered off

after every sentence.
You motioned to your friend
for some sort of drink–

I brought over a vodka tonic,
hoping you'd like it.
You looked up

at me with eyes of a startled
white heron. I said,
*you have beautiful hands,*

*they are Matisse, Renoir,*
*or Rousseau, painting the moon*
*on a clear evening.*

You thanked me
with a smile, and said
you were deaf

and read lips,
and that you loved
my French accent.

## ENGLISH AS A
## SECOND LANGUAGE

He then asked me, *Japanese,*
*Korean, Thai, or Chinese?*
I said I spoke none, although

I'd tasted their best dishes,
and I'd drunk the beers of each
country. He had spent the past

school year in Japan, learning
the strict language, savoring
the smooth spices, practicing

the classical black-ink strokes
of its characters. I learned
he would soon be twenty-one.

He was born in Mexico.
He smiled when I said I was
from the Philippine Islands.

*I want to climb out of bed*
*and find you naked, having*
*been tantalized by our long*

*bilingual exchanges.*
We spoke intimate Spanish
during the warmest moments

of our eight-hour encounter,
sharing favorite authors–
I unbuttoned his tight blue

Kawabata, he undid
my Carlos Fuentes, I slid
my hands on his beautiful

Mishima, he sighed into
my shoulder, trembled as he
felt my Octavio Paz

brush against his sculpted thigh.

# FOR MY FRIEND WHO COMPLAINS HE CAN'T DANCE AND HAS A SEVERE CASE OF WRITER'S BLOCK

Then, take this tambourine
inside the sheep barn,

listen to the anaconda's intestines,
the shark's walking stick,

learn the river insect's secret
neon calligraphy,

swim through Frida Khalo's hair
and come out smelling like orchids,

lift your appetite
towards the certified blue turtle,

feast on Garcia Lorca's leather shoes
and taste the sun, the worms of Andalusia,

don't hesitate in front of a donut,
a ferris wheel, the crab nebula,

excavate diamond-eyed demons,
Chaucer's liver, Minoan helmets,

paste Anne Sexton's face on a $1,000 bill
and purchase a dozen metaphors,

beware of the absolute scorpion,
the iguana with the limping leg,

permit indwelling, white words around the eyes,
the confrontation of windows,

never feed your towel to the alligator,
he will eat you and eat you and eat you.

# I FOUND ORPHEUS LEVITATING

above the hood of an illegally parked red Toyota Corolla
on Mabini Street. He was tired of all that descending
into and ascending from those pretentious
*New Yorker* and *Atlantic Monthly* poems.
He asked me to give him new clothes so I dressed him
in an old barong tagalog and some black pants.
Because he wanted new friends in a new land, I introduced
him to Kapitan Kidlat, our local comic book hero.
But after a few whips of that lightning bolt, Orpheus
recognized Kidlat as Zeus in another clever disguise.
So, I took him to Mt. Makiling where Malakas & Maganda
(the mythical first Filipino man and woman) live
in a mansion with an Olympic-size swimming pool.
He said Maganda's aquiline features remind him
of Eurydice and Malakas has the solid torso
of a younger Apollo. He asked me to translate
the word, *threesome* into Tagalog.
Malakas & Maganda agreed and they stripped
Orpheus of his clothes as they led him
to their giant bamboo bed.
I waited outside in the car all afternoon before he emerged
from the mansion smelling of Sampaguitas and Ylang-Ylang.
He was hungry so we drove to the nearest
Kamayan restaurant where he learned
how to eat rice and pork abobo with his bare hands.
*"It's wonderful! This was the way it used to be.*
*When the industrial revolution happened, all of us on Mt. Olympus*
*suddenly had forks and knives appear in our hands. We used*
*them as garden tools at first."* Afterwards, he wanted to drink
and go dancing. I paid the hundred-peso cover charge
for both of us at the Hobbit House in Ermita. The first
thing he did in the dark, smoky bar was trip over
one of the dwarf waiters, all the waiters were dwarfs. *"I'm sorry,*
*I couldn't see. It feels as if I had just walked into a Fellini film."*

He placed his hands in front of him as if he were pushing
back a glass wall. *"No, No, I'm not in a movie,*
*I'm inside a fucking poem!*
*I can see the poet's scrunched-up face on the other side*
*of the computer screen!"* I told Orpheus to shut up
or the bouncers, who were not the same size as the waiters,
would throw us out of the bar. We sat
in a booth across from each other and ordered double
shots of Tanduay Rum. I asked him if he understood
the concept of "the willing suspension of disbelief."
I asked him to look me straight
in the face before he ran out into the street.

## THE MOON IS THE
## MIRROR OF TIME

*"Come on moon, come sit on my lap."*
*—Athena Michelle*

My niece is two and talks with the moon.
Perhaps, her name should have been *Selene,*
the Greek word for moon which conjures up
the nocturnal beauty of that daughter of Hyperion,
and sister of Helios and Eos. But I am reminded
of her disastrous affair with Endymion,
the shepherd boy who refused Selene's love,
forcing her to surreptitiously visit his body, caress
his dreams only when he was asleep. Now
we don't want *that* kind of fate
(though a subject tragic enough to inspire Keats)
to be thrust upon my niece the rest of her evenings.

*Luna* is the Spanish word for moon containing two
syllables, two pieces which Jorge Luis Borges thought
"were too much," compared to the monosyllabic
*lua* of the Portuguese, and *lune* of the French—
descended from the Mediterranean dignity
of Latin. But the word that comes to mind
when my niece brings her ruddy-brown face
to nibble on my nose, is the Tagalog *buwan.*
I picture early Filipinos by some starry seaside hamlet
pointing to the night sky, saying,
*ooooooh, aaaaaah—booo, waaan—buwan!*

Borges says that there is a Persian metaphor
*the moon is the mirror of time.*
This brings me to the thought of Athena's father
who is seated in front of a video camera,

who needs to leave a healthy, animated image
of himself for his daughter when, in time,
she turns twelve, thirteen, or fifteen.

My niece's father is in the last stages of AIDS:
white cell blood count at thirty, opportunistic
infections clinging to his throat and everything else
below his neck. I can't help but compare
him to *la luna, la lua, la lune, ang buwan,*
the moon which is the mirror of time
my niece will see on a television screen
when she is ready to know about why . . . .

I think it is perfectly normal that my niece
should talk to the moon, that she would be considered
a lunatic through this behavior. It's really her father
she could be yearning for—a moon that is forever
present, forever distant. But for her two-year-old mind,
a moon close enough, small enough to fit on her lap.

## about the author

Nick Carbó was born in 1964 in Legazpi, Albay in the
Philippines. He received an M.F.A. in Creative Writing
from Sarah Lawrence College and has served as Resident
Poet at Bucknell University and Writer-in-Residence at
The American University. He is the editor of *Returning A
Borrowed Tongue: An Anthology of Contemporary Filipino and
Filipino-American Poetry* (Coffee House Press 1996). He is
married to the beautiful poet Denise Duhamel.